SUDOKUGRAMS

Alan Stillson & Frank Longo

STERLING

New York / London
www.sterlingpublishing.com

2   4   6   8   10   9   7   5   3   1

Published by Sterling Publishing Co., Inc.
387 Park Avenue South, New York, NY 10016
© 2008 by Alan Stillson & Frank Longo
Distributed in Canada by Sterling Publishing
^{c}/o Canadian Manda Group, 165 Dufferin Street
Toronto, Ontario, Canada M6K 3H6
Distributed in the United Kingdom by GMC Distribution Services
Castle Place, 166 High Street, Lewes, East Sussex, England BN7 1XU
Distributed in Australia by Capricorn Link (Australia) Pty. Ltd.
P.O. Box 704, Windsor, NSW 2756, Australia

Sterling ISBN-13: 978-1-4027-4641-3
ISBN-10: 1-4027-4641-5

For information about custom editions, special sales, premium and
corporate purchases, please contact Sterling Special Sales
Department at 800-805-5489 or specialsales@sterlingpublishing.com.

CONTENTS

SUDOKUGRAMS IN A NUTSHELL

The rules of Sudokugrams are simple:

1. Fill in the empty squares using the letters given beneath the grid, using each given letter only once.
2. Make sure there are no repeated letters in any of the rows, columns, or heavily outlined 2×2 sections
3. Form twelve different sets of four letters in the rows, columns, and 2×2 sections so that each set can be anagrammed into a common word. Abbreviations are not allowed. For a complete list of acceptable words, see page 127.

Here is a sample puzzle and its solution.

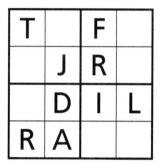

Rows: FATE, JURY, IDOL, RASP.
Columns: TOUR, JADE, FIRS,
PLAY. Boxes: JUTE, FRAY, ROAD,
SLIP.

SUDOKUGRAMS IN DETAIL

Sudokugrams are puzzles that combine the logic of sudoku with the wordplay of anagrams. When you solve a sudoku puzzle, you place numbers in squares in such a way that there are no repeating numbers in rows, columns, or 3×3 sections. Sudokugrams have the same no-repeat rule, but while you have fewer squares to fill in, you must also be able to rearrange the letters in each row, column, and 2×2 section into words. Offensive words are not allowed, and no obscure words are needed to complete the puzzles. Here are some more comparisons between Sudokugrams and traditional sudoku puzzles:

	SUDOKUGRAMS	SUDOKU
Grid size	4×4	9×9
Number of squares	16	81
Section size	2×2	3×3
Characters used	Letters	Numbers
Number of givens	Maximum of 10	Maximum of 30
Difficulty	Varies	Varies
Solving time	5–15 minutes	10+ minutes
Skills needed	Logic and wordplay	Logic

For the purpose of this book, we took the list of all the allowable four-letter Scrabble words (over 4,000), and chose the ones that appeared in *Webster's II Dictionary, Third Edition* (Berkley Books). We selected this dictionary because it is small, but contained nearly all the words that we considered common. After compiling the list, we noticed a lot of obscure currencies, some words that traditionally are not allowed in crossword puzzles because of their topic, and a few other strange words, so we deleted 64 words. For every word we took out, we added two words that didn't appear in the dictionary but that we felt were common (many of these were short forms of longer words, like *comp* and *spec*). If you're not sure if a word is acceptable or not, you can check the complete list of 2,052 allowable words on page 127.

Some sets of four letters often have more than one anagram. So, for example, you may use either *cape* or *pace* to anagram the letter group "*acep*." However, no two sets in a puzzle can contain the same four letters, so if one row has *acep*, then no other row, column, or 2×2 section can contain those same four letters.

All puzzles were tested by a computer program specially written for Sudokugrams to assure unique solutions (not counting different anagrams of the same set of letters) within the scope of allowable words.

However, if you use words that go beyond our list, it is possible that other solutions exist. In other words, if you stick to our common words, your answer grid will match ours, but the anagrams listed may differ when there's more than one way to rearrange the four letters.

Here are some solving tips to help you get started:

1. Start with squares where only one available letter in the letter pool can form a word in a row, column, or 2×2 section without repeating any letters.

2. Cross off letters from the letter pool as they are placed.

3. Look for squares where two possible remaining letters can be placed. Write them lightly in pencil and see which letter leads to a dead end. Then select the letter that works.

4. If there's an uncommon letter in the grid, then the squares in its row, column, or section are often a good place to start. Similarly, if an uncommon letter is in the letter pool, there probably aren't many squares in which it will work.

5. Be alert for words that start with a vowel or end in a vowel other than *e*. Since most words start with a consonant or end with a consonant or an *e*, it's easy to forget about words like *menu* and *onus* as opposed to words like *park* or *bone*. So, before rejecting a four-letter combination like *inot*, look at it more closely and you'll find it can be anagrammed as *into*.

Here's a step-by-step walk-through of how to solve a puzzle.

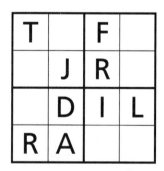

The square in the second column of the first row must contain E since no other letter leads to a word in column 2 (JADE). We now have the grid shown on the next page.

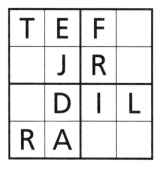

A A̶ O P S U Y

The square in the third column of the fourth row must contain S since only A and S lead to a word in column 3 (FAIR or FIRS), but A can't be chosen because there's already an A in the fourth row. We now have:

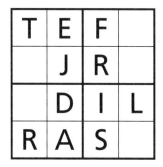

A A̶ O P S̶ U Y

This leaves A as the only possibility for the fourth column of the first row. The word formed in the top row is FATE, FEAT, or FETA. Remember that while there can be more than one anagram for some four-letter combinations, there's only one way to place the letters into the grid to make everything work.

In the first column of the second row, only U works (JUTE) for the upper left section. Once the U is in place, the last letter of the second row must be Y to make JURY in row 2 and FRAY in the upper right. We now have:

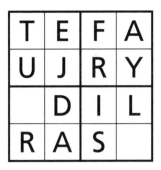

All that's left to place are O and P. In the third row, the missing square has to be an O (to make IDOL in row 3, TOUR or ROUT in column 1, and ROAD in the lower-left 2×2 region). That leaves the P for the remaining square. A quick check verifies that it makes words in its row (PARS, RAPS, RASP, or SPAR), column (PLAY), and region (LIPS, LISP, or SLIP). The final answer is shown below.

T	E	F	A
U	J	R	Y
O	D	I	L
R	A	S	P

Rows: FATE, JURY, IDOL, SPAR.
Columns: TOUR, JADE, FIRS, PLAY. Boxes: JUTE, FRAY, ROAD, SLIP.

Acknowledgments
Alan Stillson and Frank Longo thank the National Puzzlers League, under the leadership of Will Shortz, for maintaining an atmosphere where puzzle authors and solvers work together to produce and perfect books like *Sudokugrams*. Within the League, an extra special hat-tip goes to Francis Heaney for some great suggestions in structuring the puzzles to make them more solvable. And a big thank-you to Corey Kosak for the computer program.

Alan Stillson also acknowledges Bruce D'Ambrosio, leader of the West Los Angeles Scrabble Club, for initial suggestions on structuring the puzzles.

The Word People Panel

To make sure these puzzles were solvable, we assembled a testing panel consisting of "word people"—folks who love word puzzles or games and who are familiar with sudoku. Many thanks to the Word People Panel members: Jody Carlson, Karen Cooper, Bruce D'Ambrosio, Chris Dudlak, Jonathan Elliott, Jay French, Susie Gelfand, Eliot Kieval, Michael Langley, G. Christom Larsin, Vince Lobuzzetta, Jo Ann Lynn, Dr. Robert J. Meier, Chuck Murphy, Brett Radlicki, Bill Siderski, Marc Spraragen, Pat Stenger, Pamela Stubblefield, Timothy J. Sullivan, Ron Sweet, and Dennis Tomlinson.

Here are two more sample puzzles. The answers are on page 10.

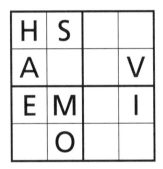

A E G R T T W Y

C E F K R S T U

H	S	R	E
A	W	Y	V
E	M	T	I
T	O	A	G

Rows: HERS, WAVY, TIME, GOAT.
Columns: HEAT, MOWS, TRAY, GIVE. Boxes: WASH, VERY, TOME, GAIT.

A	D	R	K
R	T	F	O
I	E	T	C
P	N	U	S

Rows: DARK, FORT, CITE, SPUN.
Columns: PAIR, DENT, TURF, SOCK. Boxes: DART, FORK, PINE, CUTS.

F		E	
	D	P	O
A			S
G	R		T

C I K M N U

C		D	
R	P		A
	E		W
U	H		N

I L O S T Y

3

Y		E	R
L			
	N	A	T
I	T		S

C F K O U W

4

Y	L		O
		T	A
A		N	
S		I	R

D E H P T W

Answers, page 86

5

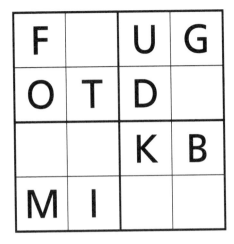

F		U	G
O	T	D	
		K	B
M	I		

A C E L N R

6

	D		M
Y		T	S
R		K	I
A	E		

B C L N O U

7

B			P
R	G		C
E	T		I
	H	O	

A L M N U W

8

			A
I	C	E	
V	A	R	
	L	O	G

E L N O R Y

Answers, page 87

L	M		A
	E		R
	T	I	M
O		C	

E K P R S T

10

N		D	
E	T	A	
P	S		A
	D	E	

I L O R U V

B		S	
M	C		U
		W	
L	E		T

A H I K N O P

D			
M			A
	C	L	E
N	K		H

I O P S T U Y

Answers, page 88

	O	S	
N			I
A		C	
M		U	D

B E K P R T Y

A		I	
	E	N	
S		L	O
	U		C

D G H K R T V

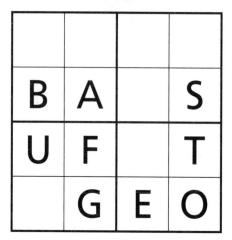

I K L N P R W

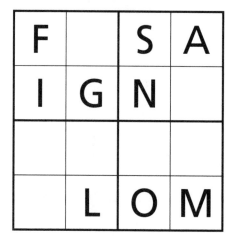

B C E P R T U

Answers, page 89

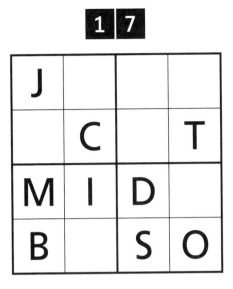

J			
	C		T
M	I	D	
B		S	O

A E K L N P R

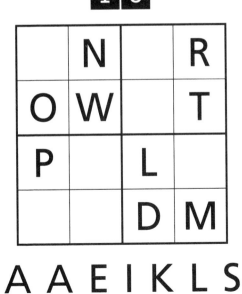

	N		R
O	W		T
P		L	
		D	M

A A E I K L S

	A	N	G
	S		
L			P
T	D	E	

E F I I O R W

	K	E	
E			I
	B	S	E
H			L

A A C D O T T

Answers, page 90

21

T		O	N
A	L		E
E		R	
	A		

A B D E E K Z

22

		O	
B	E		L
		K	O
E	O	R	

A B C N R W Z

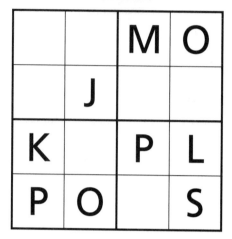

A A C E K S W

24

T	B	E	
	O		D
A		B	
	S		T

A B E I J L U

Answers, page 91

2 5

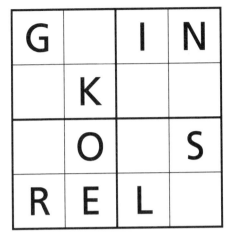

G		I	N
	K		
	O		S
R	E	L	

A B C H P U W

2 6

P	M		
U		R	S
N			D
	A	W	

B E G I K L O

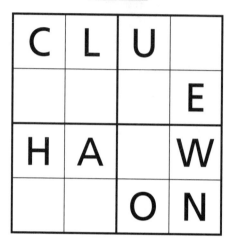

C	L	U	
			E
H	A		W
		O	N

D I K M P R S

2 8

	H	S	O
			C
T	A		
H		U	D

B E I N R W Z

Answers, page 92

N			I
W		S	R
	P	T	M
		U	

A B D E F L O

K		H	W
	B	S	
E		D	
P	R		

A I L M N O Y

3 1

	S		A
T			H
U	E	T	
S			M

B D I J O R S

3 2

		G	N
B	H	A	
	E		O
N			R

D E M S T U W

Answers, page 93

F	A	W	
			N
N	O		B
	C		E

A D E I M N T

	G	S	
	L		O
	B	A	
D		N	W

E F H L O U W

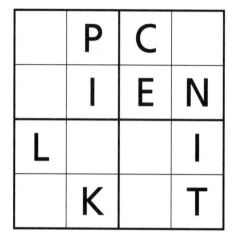

A C D I K P S

36

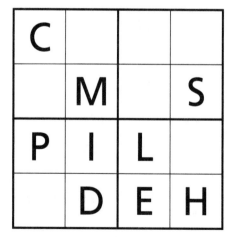

A B L M S T U

Answers, page 94

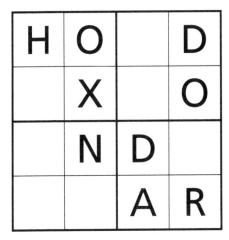

A D E N S W Y

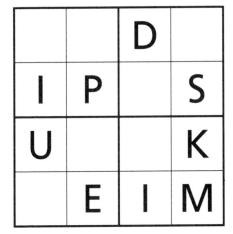

A D L Q R U W

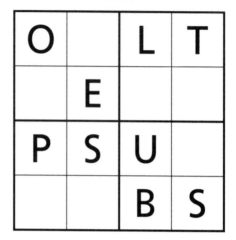

A C E H J K T

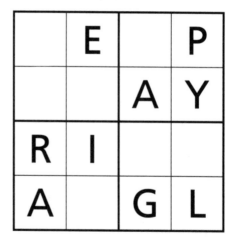

F N N O S T V

Answers, page 95

	R		I
	D	P	S
L			
K	N		E

A A C I M T V

S	E		I
		N	R
G	O		L
R			

A B D E I K W

43

	U	S	
R		P	
	B	R	S
S	O		

A E G J L U Y

44

		N	E
		A	
R		I	T
D	U		O

F L L M O P P

Answers, page 96

E	D	L	
	I	O	C
	P		L
A			

E F I M N S U

4 6

	A	R	
L		T	I
	P		
E	O	H	

A D L M M S U

4 7

	S	I	H
E		P	
A			B
D	E		

G K N O S U W

4 8

L			D
U	T		
	I	L	
R		O	T

A C E E F F G

 Answers, page 97

E		T	S
D			
	A		T
B		L	I

E L M O O R V

5 0

L	S	N	
	D	O	
A			
	E	U	P

E H I L R S W

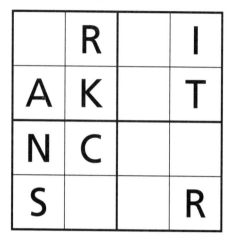

	R		I
A	K		T
N	C		
S			R

B E G L O T U

T	R		A
		N	
I	L	A	
	O		M

C D E K K S W

Answers, page 98

53

	E		H
D	N	A	
	I	O	N
		S	

A E K M R R U

54

G	L		
	N	B	
S		A	
R	I		T

A D E K M O U

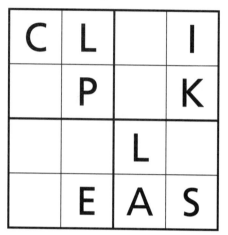

A E J K O P T

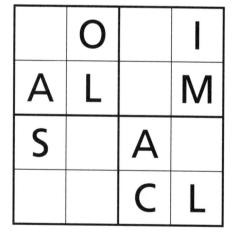

D D E P T U V

Answers, page 99

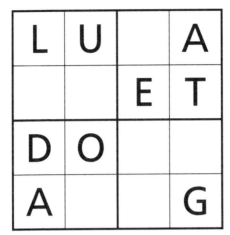

L	U		A
		E	T
D	O		
A			G

G L M N O S W

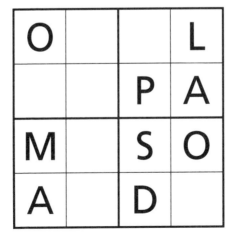

O			L
		P	A
M		S	O
A		D	

B E I L R R W

S		H	
	P	C	O
			M
	N	R	E

D E F I O U W

G	O		
	N	D	
		B	R
L	E	I	

A C E F M O R

Answers, page 100

61

	L	O	
	T		A
P			H
	I	S	R

E L P S T U W

62

		D	
R	S		A
E	L	M	
		S	P

B E I M O O U

H		P	
	I	G	N
		A	D
A	M		

E I N S W Y Z

		I	S
R			P
B	E		
D		W	A

E G M N O S Z

Answers, page 101

U	D	P	
E	R		
	O	Y	A

A E K L M R S T

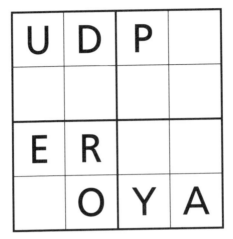

6 6

F			A
I		E	L
H			
	P		C

A H L M R S T U

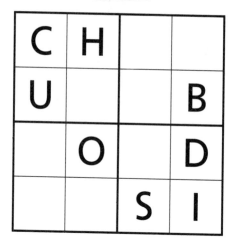

C	H		
U			B
	O		D
		S	I

B E M N P R S U

---

6 8

H		E	O
M			
		P	
N	I	A	

G I L S S T U Y

Answers, page 102

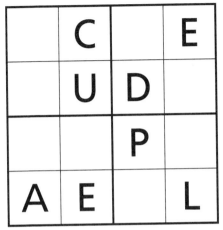

	C		E
	U	D	
		P	
A	E		L

A A H L M O R S

C		T	N
P		D	I
O			L

A E E K O R R W

	L	A	E
			R
T		D	
	M		P

A E G I L O P Y

	E	G	
N		I	
I			E
	P	N	

A E L S T V W Y

Answers, page 103

		N	
U		D	
	C	I	E
A			R

A A B E K L M T

	A	P	R
		E	
P		S	
	H		E

D I O S T T U X

I	E	U	
D			
	H	O	
	N		T

E E L M R S T W

N	S		
	T	O	D
		C	
		R	A

E E F G I L O W

Answers, page 104

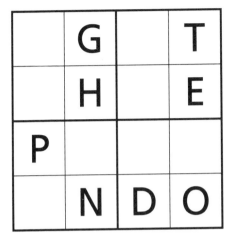

	G		T
	H		E
P			
	N	D	O

A C E S S U V W

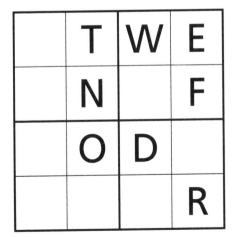

	T	W	E
	N		F
	O	D	
			R

A D E H I I L N

79

	E		A
	R	E	T
K	A	R	

B C I L L M O W

80

	E	O	
O		G	L
S			
		A	T

E F I L R R T W

Answers, page 105

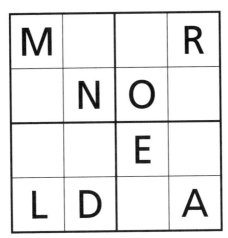

D E G L N O T U

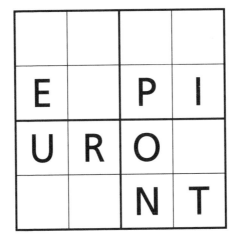

A C D E F M S S

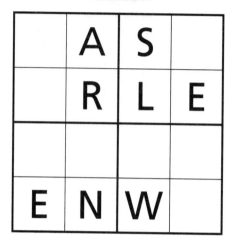

	A	S	
	R	L	E
E	N	W	

A G H N T T W Y

84

P		O	N
	B	N	
D		A	E

D E H I R R T U

Answers, page 106

N	S		E
		D	
R			
	I	T	N

A E G M O R W W

8 6

	A		R
		H	A
P	I		
	T		S

E E N O R S W Y

87

T		O	
	M		E
			P
	E	L	A

I I L L N N O S

88

S	P	A	
			L
		R	I
	N	E	

D E I I K T T T

89

A	L		O
C			L
			C
O		A	

D E E F S T T V

90

E		A	
	O	G	E
B			
A			R

E F G M O S S Z

		E	A
E			
P			M
L		T	P

A C D E H K O W

9 2

		U	
Y		L	
	T		S
		G	A

A E F N O P P X

Answers, page 108

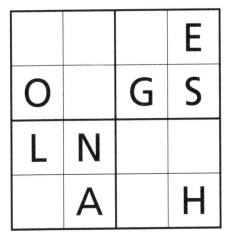

			E
O		G	S
L	N		
	A		H

A B D O O T W Y

9 4

	N	U	
	E		
N	D		A
O		M	

A E F L R S S V

95

G	I	D	
T			I
	F		L
R			

E F I N O R T W

96

N			D
		B	R
I			E
	T	C	

A A D H K K L U

Answers, page 109

97

		T	
A	M		N
	I	D	
E		L	

E E O R S T W Z

98

	S	U	T
	R		D
		D	A
B			

A J L N R S U Y

	T		E
S		O	
A		S	P
	I		

A C H H L N T Y

	L	I	
A			P
	A		R
		W	I

A D E E F K N S

Answers, page 110

101

	S	G	
I			S
W		V	
N	R		

A D E I O O T W

102

H	P		S
O			
	C		
P		Y	L

A E E N O R S U

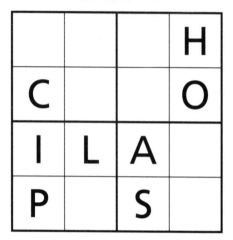

A E E K L M R W

104

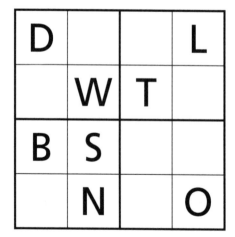

A A E O P R U Y

Answers, page 111

1 0 5

		N	T
	O	I	
D	B		
	M		A

A C E L P S U Y

1 0 6

	Y		
		N	I
E		W	
O	P		A

A C E M R R S V

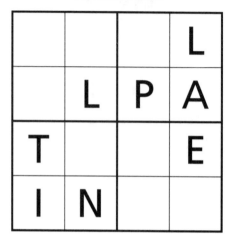

			L
	L	P	A
T			E
I	N		

A G R S S U U Y

108

P	O		
		W	N
	D		O
W	E		

A E K M N P S T

Answers, page 112

109

P		C	H
	I	L	
A	R		S

A E E M N O T U

110

	S		E
B		O	
			M
L	A		I

A D D F G N O R

111

N	L		E
			P
			S
U	D	E	

A H I J K N O R

112

	H		A
R			
M	P		L
	R	V	

A C E E E I O V

113

	I		O
N			S
	S	R	
	H		I

A B D E K L L U

114

A		E	
	T		I
B		S	
	N	T	

D H K L O U V W

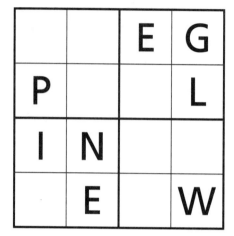

ACHKMORU

115

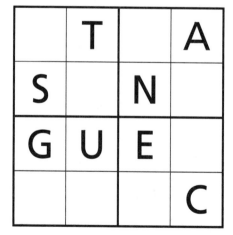

AHILNOPW

Answers, page 114

	M	E	
D			I
		T	S
N			O

A B F G L L R U

R			
	T	B	L
		N	
C		M	A

A C E K L O U Y

		E	L
R			O
U	S		C
	G		

A B I I K N P T

120

A		R	
		H	U
F	O		S
L			

C E E G I K P T

Answers, page 115

121

N	R		O
I		E	
			T
S		A	

C G H I L P V W

122

	T		P
M		R	
		L	C
	E		A

A D E F I K O R

D		G	A
O		L	
		S	P
E			

A B C E P R T U

| 1 | 2 | 4 |

H			U
	A	K	N
	R	N	
C			

E G I I M S S T

Answers, page 116

125

	L	O	S
P	S	L	
	I	D	

A A E K T T W Y

126

		A	R
N			I
R		O	
T		M	

A E E G G S T Y

I		L	
B		S	
	U	E	
	R		M

A A K L O R S W

P		S	
	N		R
		E	
A	R		T

A B G I S T U Y

Answers, page 117

129

	E		A
T			
A	L		C
	I	D	

B D E K L O S Z

130

B	R	G	
	I		S
		U	
T			B

A E F L L M O S

131

S			
		B	R
N		U	
	M	R	E

A A E S T T V Y

132

		F	E
T			O
	S		B
E	N		

A A C H L R T Y

Answers, page 118

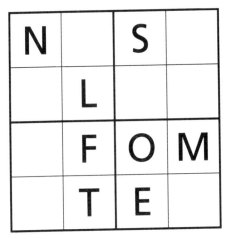

A I I K L P R W

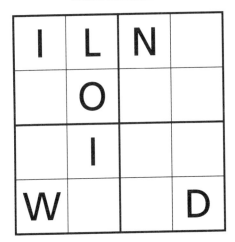

A B E H K R R T U

135

	N	T	A
	I		E
	P		T

A E E E F L L R X

136

N		A	
		H	E
E			
O	D		

A E L N P T V Y Z

Answers, page 119

1 3 7

			O
N		I	
C			S
	L	U	

A B E E J N R T X

1 3 8

			O
P	I	E	
	N		
	D	S	

B C H H I K R U W

139

P			I
	B	H	S
	E	O	

A A G J K M N R R

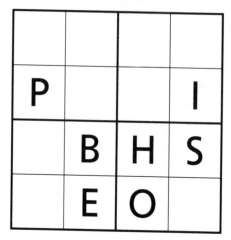

140

		L	
P		C	
	E		M
A	D		

A B E L N O T U Y

Answers, page 120

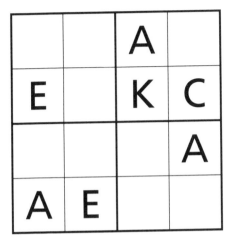

B H N R T T V W Y

142

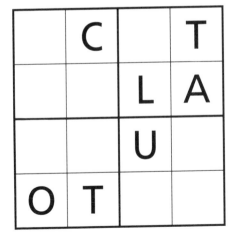

A D E F G I R S Y

	L		B
F		S	
B			R
		A	

A A C C E L M O U

1 4 4

	O	A	
E			
S		D	
		M	I

H I K K N N P T Y

Answers, page 121

G		L	A
	O		
	S		N
	P		

A E E F I N R W X

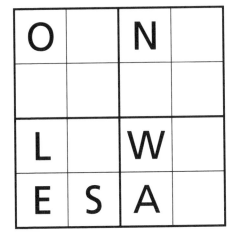

O		N	
L		W	
E	S	A	

A B H K M O O T Y

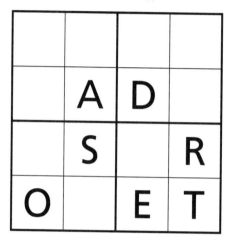

B E I J L M N O V

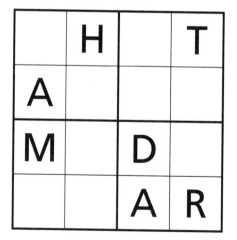

E I N O O S T T U

Answers, page 122

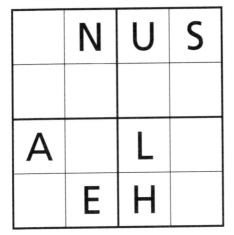

	N	U	S
A		L	
	E	H	

B D D I I K L O S

1 5 0

S			
			H
	B	N	E
		A	

E G G L M N O S S U

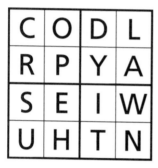

F	U	E	M
N	D	P	O
A	C	K	S
G	R	I	T

1

Rows: FUME, POND, SACK, GRIT.
Columns: FANG, CURD, PIKE, MOST. Boxes: FUND, POEM, CRAG, SKIT.

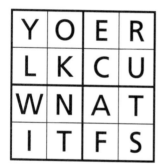

C	O	D	L
R	P	Y	A
S	E	I	W
U	H	T	N

2

Rows: COLD, PRAY, WISE, HUNT. Columns: CURS, HOPE, TIDY, LAWN. Boxes: CROP, LADY, HUES, TWIN.

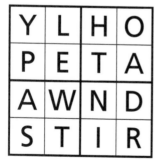

Y	O	E	R
L	K	C	U
W	N	A	T
I	T	F	S

3

Rows: YORE, LUCK, WANT, FIST. Columns: WILY, KNOT, FACE, RUST. Boxes: YOLK, CURE, TWIN, FAST.

Y	L	H	O
P	E	T	A
A	W	N	D
S	T	I	R

4

Rows: HOLY, TAPE, WAND, STIR. Columns: PAYS, WELT, THIN, ROAD. Boxes: YELP, OATH, SWAT, RIND.

5

Rows: GULF, TROD, BANK, MICE.
Columns: FOAM, LINT, DUCK,
BERG. Boxes: LOFT, DRUG,
MAIN, BECK.

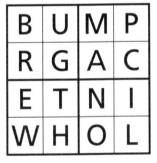

6

Rows: DUMB, TOYS, RINK, LACE.
Columns: BRAY, DONE, TUCK,
SLIM. Boxes: BODY, MUST,
NEAR, LICK.

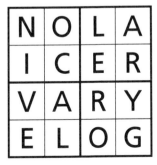

7

Rows: BUMP, CRAG, TINE,
HOWL. Columns: BREW, THUG,
MOAN, CLIP. Boxes: GRUB,
CAMP, WHET, LION.

8

Rows: LOAN, RICE, VARY, LOGE.
Columns: VINE, COAL, ROLE,
GRAY. Boxes: COIN, REAL, VEAL,
GORY.

L	M	P	A
T	E	K	R
S	T	I	M
O	R	C	E

9

Rows: LAMP, TREK, MIST, CORE.
Columns: LOST, TERM, PICK, MARE. Boxes: MELT, PARK, SORT, MICE.

N	U	D	O
E	T	A	L
P	S	R	A
I	D	E	V

10

Rows: UNDO, LATE, SPAR, DIVE. Columns: PINE, DUST, READ, OVAL. Boxes: TUNE, LOAD, DIPS, RAVE.

B	O	S	P
M	C	H	U
I	K	W	N
L	E	A	T

11

Rows: BOPS, MUCH, WINK, LATE. Columns: LIMB, COKE, WASH, PUNT. Boxes: COMB, PUSH, LIKE, WANT.

D	U	T	Y
M	P	S	A
I	C	L	E
N	K	O	H

12

Rows: DUTY, MAPS, LICE, HONK. Columns: MIND, PUCK, SLOT, YEAH. Boxes: DUMP, STAY, NICK, HOLE.

Y	O	S	B
N	P	T	I
A	K	C	E
M	R	U	D

1 3

Rows: BOYS, PINT, CAKE, DRUM. Columns: MANY, PORK, CUTS, BIDE. Boxes: PONY, BITS, MARK, CUED.

A	H	I	R
V	E	N	D
S	G	L	O
T	U	K	C

1 4

Rows: HAIR, VEND, LOGS, TUCK. Columns: VAST, HUGE, LINK, CORD. Boxes: HAVE, RIND, GUST, LOCK.

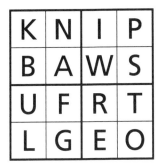

1 5

Rows: PINK, SWAB, TURF, LOGE. Columns: BULK, FANG, WIRE, STOP. Boxes: BANK, WISP, GULF, TORE.

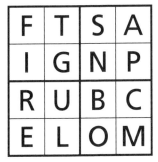

1 6

Rows: FAST, PING, CURB, MOLE. Columns: FIRE, GLUT, SNOB, CAMP. Boxes: GIFT, SNAP, RULE, COMB.

J	K	E	R
A	C	P	T
M	I	D	N
B	L	S	O

1 7

Rows: JERK, PACT, MIND, LOBS.
Columns: JAMB, LICK, SPED, TORN. Boxes: JACK, PERT, LIMB, NODS.

K	N	A	R
O	W	S	T
P	A	L	I
E	L	D	M

1 8

Rows: RANK, STOW, PAIL, MELD.
Columns: POKE, LAWN, LADS, TRIM. Boxes: KNOW, STAR, PEAL, MILD.

F	A	N	G
E	S	I	R
L	O	W	P
T	D	E	I

1 9

Rows: FANG, RISE, PLOW, TIDE.
Columns: FELT, SODA, WINE, GRIP. Boxes: SAFE, GRIN, TOLD, WIPE.

A	K	E	T
E	C	D	I
T	B	S	E
H	A	O	L

2 0

Rows: TAKE, DICE, BEST, HALO.
Columns: HEAT, BACK, DOES, TILE. Boxes: CAKE, TIDE, BATH, SOLE.

T	E	O	N
A	L	Z	E
E	K	R	A
B	A	E	D

2 1

Rows: TONE, ZEAL, RAKE, BEAD. Columns: BEAT, LAKE, ZERO, DEAN. Boxes: LATE, ZONE, BAKE, READ.

A	R	O	B
B	E	W	L
N	Z	K	O
E	O	R	C

2 2

Rows: BOAR, BLEW, ZONK, CORE. Columns: BEAN, ZERO, WORK, BLOC. Boxes: BEAR, BLOW, ZONE, ROCK.

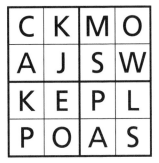

2 3

Rows: MOCK, JAWS, KELP, SOAP. Columns: PACK, JOKE, MAPS, SLOW. Boxes: JACK, MOWS, POKE, SLAP.

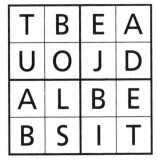

2 4

Rows: BEAT, JUDO, ABLE, BITS. Columns: TUBA, LOBS, JIBE, DATE. Boxes: BOUT, JADE, SLAB, BITE.

G	W	I	N
A	K	C	H
B	O	P	S
R	E	L	U

Rows: WING, HACK, BOPS, RULE. Columns: GRAB, WOKE, CLIP, SHUN. Boxes: GAWK, CHIN, BORE, PLUS.

P	M	G	I
U	L	R	S
N	B	O	D
K	A	W	E

2 6

Rows: GIMP, SLUR, BOND, WEAK. Columns: PUNK, BALM, GROW, SIDE. Boxes: PLUM, RIGS, BANK, OWED.

C	L	U	K
I	P	D	E
H	A	S	W
R	M	O	N

2 7

Rows: LUCK, PIED, WASH, MORN. Columns: RICH, PALM, DUOS, KNEW. Boxes: CLIP, DUKE, HARM, SOWN.

W	H	S	O
I	Z	N	C
T	A	B	R
H	E	U	D

2 8

Rows: SHOW, ZINC, BRAT, HUED. Columns: WITH, HAZE, SNUB, CORD. Boxes: WHIZ, CONS, HEAT, DRUB.

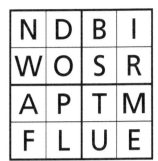

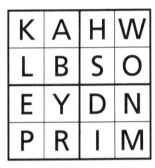

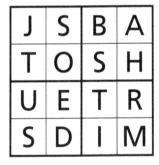

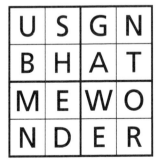

2 9

Rows: BIND, ROWS, TAMP, FLUE.
Columns: FAWN, PLOD, STUB,
MIRE. Boxes: DOWN, RIBS,
FLAP, MUTE.

3 0

Rows: HAWK, LOBS, DENY,
PRIM. Columns: KELP, BRAY,
DISH, MOWN. Boxes: BALK,
SHOW, PREY, MIND.

3 1

Rows: JABS, SHOT, TRUE, DIMS.
Columns: JUTS, DOES, BITS,
HARM. Boxes: JOTS, BASH,
SUED, TRIM.

3 2

Rows: SNUG, BATH, MEOW,
NERD. Columns: NUMB, SHED,
WAGE, TORN. Boxes: BUSH,
GNAT, MEND, WORE.

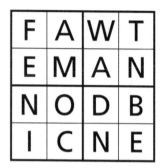

Rows: WAFT, MEAN, BOND, NICE. Columns: FINE, COMA, WAND, BENT. Boxes: FAME, WANT, COIN, BEND.

3 4

Rows: GUSH, FLOW, ABLE, DOWN. Columns: FEUD, GLOB, SWAN, HOWL. Boxes: GULF, SHOW, BODE, LAWN.

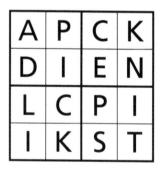

3 5

Rows: PACK, DINE, CLIP, SKIT. Columns: DIAL, PICK, SPEC, KNIT. Boxes: PAID, NECK, LICK, PITS.

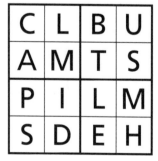

3 6

Rows: CLUB, MAST, LIMP, SHED. Columns: CAPS, MILD, BELT, MUSH. Boxes: CLAM, STUB, DIPS, HELM.

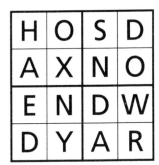

3 7

Rows: SHOD, AXON, WEND, YARD. Columns: HEAD, ONYX, SAND, WORD. Boxes: HOAX, NODS, DENY, DRAW.

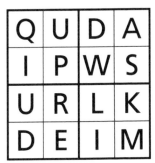

3 8

Rows: QUAD, WISP, LURK, DIME. Columns: QUID, PURE, WILD, MASK. Boxes: QUIP, WADS, RUDE, MILK.

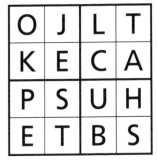

3 9

Rows: JOLT, CAKE, PUSH, BEST. Columns: POKE, JEST, CLUB, HATS. Boxes: JOKE, TALC, PEST, BUSH.

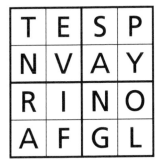

4 0

Rows: PEST, NAVY, IRON, FLAG. Columns: RANT, FIVE, SANG, PLOY. Boxes: VENT, PAYS, FAIR, LONG.

Rows: TRIM, PADS, VIAL, NECK.
Columns: TALK, RIND, CAMP, VIES. Boxes: DART, IMPS, LINK, CAVE.

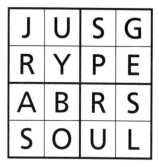

Rows: SIDE, RANK, GLOB, WIRE.
Columns: RAGS, WOKE, BIND, RILE. Boxes: SAKE, RIND, GROW, BILE.

Rows: JUGS, PREY, BARS, SOUL.
Columns: JARS, BUOY, SPUR, LEGS. Boxes: JURY, PEGS, BOAS, SLUR.

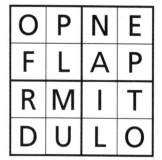

Rows: OPEN, FLAP, TRIM, LOUD.
Columns: FORD, PLUM, NAIL, POET. Boxes: FLOP, PANE, DRUM, TOIL.

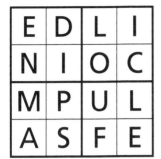

Rows: LIED, COIN, PLUM, SAFE.
Columns: MEAN, DIPS, FOUL, LICE. Boxes: DINE, COIL, MAPS, FUEL.

4 6

Rows: DRAM, LIST, PUMA, HOLE. Columns: MELD, SOAP, HURT, MAIL. Boxes: LADS, TRIM, MOPE, HAUL.

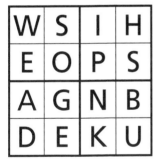

4 7

Rows: WISH, POSE, BANG, DUKE. Columns: WADE, GOES, PINK, BUSH. Boxes: WOES, SHIP, AGED, BUNK.

4 8

Rows: GLAD, CUTE, LIFE, FORT. Columns: RULE, GIFT, COAL, DEFT. Boxes: GLUT, ACED, FIRE, LOFT.

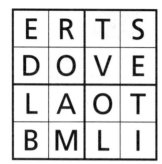

E	R	T	S
D	O	V	E
L	A	O	T
B	M	L	I

4 9

Rows: REST, DOVE, ALTO, LIMB.
Columns: BLED, ROAM, VOLT, SITE. Boxes: RODE, VEST, BALM, TOIL.

L	S	N	E
I	D	O	L
A	W	S	H
R	E	U	P

5 0

Rows: LENS, IDOL, WASH, PURE. Columns: RAIL, WEDS, ONUS, HELP. Boxes: LIDS, LONE, WEAR, PUSH.

B	R	G	I
A	K	L	T
N	C	T	E
S	O	U	R

5 1

Rows: BRIG, TALK, CENT, SOUR. Columns: BANS, ROCK, GLUT, TIRE. Boxes: BARK, GILT, CONS, TRUE.

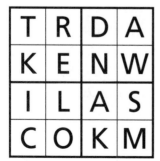

T	R	D	A
K	E	N	W
I	L	A	S
C	O	K	M

5 2

Rows: DART, KNEW, SAIL, MOCK. Columns: TICK, ROLE, DANK, SWAM. Boxes: TREK, WAND, COIL, MASK.

5 3

Rows: HEAR, DANK, IRON, MUSE. Columns: READ, MINE, SOAR, HUNK. Boxes: DEAN, HARK, MIRE, ONUS.

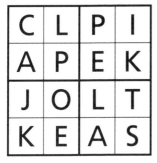

5 4

Rows: GALE, NUMB, SOAK, DIRT. Columns: RUGS, LINK, BEAD, MOAT. Boxes: LUNG, BEAM, RISK, TOAD.

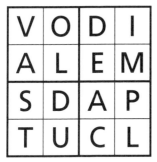

5 5

Rows: CLIP, PEAK, JOLT, SAKE. Columns: JACK, POLE, PALE, SKIT. Boxes: CLAP, PIKE, JOKE, SALT.

5 6

Rows: VOID, MEAL, PADS, CULT. Columns: VAST, LOUD, ACED, LIMP. Boxes: OVAL, DIME, DUST, CLAP.

5 7

Rows: MAUL, GETS, DOWN, GOAL. Columns: GLAD, SOUL, MEOW, TANG. Boxes: SLUG, TEAM, LOAD, GOWN.

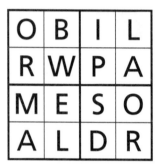

5 8

Rows: BOIL, WARP, SOME, LARD. Columns: ROAM, BLEW, DIPS, ORAL. Boxes: BROW, PAIL, MEAL, RODS.

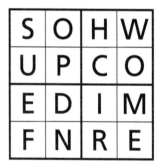

5 9

Rows: SHOW, COUP, DIME, FERN. Columns: FUSE, POND, RICH, MEOW. Boxes: SOUP, CHOW, FEND, MIRE.

6 0

Rows: FROG, DONE, CRAB, MILE. Columns: GALE, ONCE, BIRD, FORM. Boxes: GONE, FORD, LACE, BRIM.

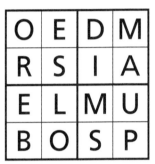

Rows: PLOW, LATE, PUSH, STIR. Columns: WEPT, LIST, SOUL, HARP. Boxes: WELT, OPAL, PITS, RUSH.

6 2

Rows: MODE, AIRS, MULE, BOPS. Columns: ROBE, SOLE, DIMS, PUMA. Boxes: ROSE, MAID, LOBE, SUMP.

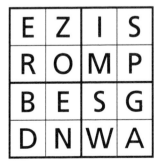

6 3

Rows: WHIP, ZING, DAYS, MEAN. Columns: HAZY, SWIM, PANG, DINE. Boxes: WHIZ, PING, YAMS, DEAN.

6 4

Rows: SIZE, ROMP, BEGS, WAND. Columns: BRED, ZONE, SWIM, GASP. Boxes: ZERO, IMPS, BEND, WAGS.

6 5

Rows: DUPE, LARK, REST, MAYO.
Columns: MULE, ROAD, SPRY, TAKE. Boxes: DUAL, PERK, MORE, STAY.

F	L	H	A
I	M	E	L
H	U	R	T
S	P	A	C

6 6

Rows: HALF, MILE, HURT, CAPS.
Columns: FISH, LUMP, HEAR, TALC. Boxes: FILM, HEAL, PUSH, CART.

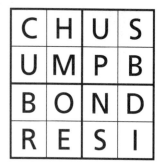

6 7

Rows: SUCH, BUMP, BOND, RISE. Columns: CURB, HOME, SPUN, BIDS. Boxes: MUCH, PUBS, BORE, DINS.

H	S	E	O
M	U	G	S
Y	T	P	I
N	I	A	L

6 8

Rows: HOSE, MUGS, PITY, NAIL.
Columns: HYMN, SUIT, PAGE, SOIL. Boxes: MUSH, GOES, TINY, PAIL.

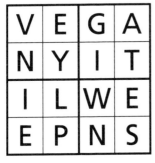

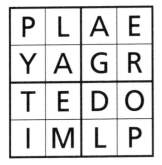

H	C	A	E
O	U	D	R
L	S	P	A
A	E	M	L

6 9

Rows: EACH, DOUR, SLAP, MEAL. Columns: HALO, CUES, DAMP, REAL. Boxes: OUCH, READ, SALE, PALM.

C	A	T	N
R	W	O	K
P	E	D	I
O	R	E	L

7 0

Rows: CANT, WORK, PIED, ROLE. Columns: CROP, WEAR, DOTE, LINK. Boxes: CRAW, KNOT, ROPE, LIED.

P	L	A	E
Y	A	G	R
T	E	D	O
I	M	L	P

7 1

Rows: PALE, GRAY, DOTE, LIMP. Columns: PITY, MEAL, GLAD, ROPE. Boxes: PLAY, GEAR, TIME, PLOD.

V	E	G	A
N	Y	I	T
I	L	W	E
E	P	N	S

7 2

Rows: GAVE, TINY, WILE, PENS. Columns: VINE, YELP, WING, SEAT. Boxes: ENVY, GAIT, PILE, NEWS.

B	E	N	A
U	A	D	L
T	C	I	E
A	K	M	R

7 3

Rows: BEAN, LAUD, CITE, MARK.
Columns: TUBA, CAKE, MIND,
REAL. Boxes: BEAU, LAND,
TACK, MIRE.

T	A	P	R
I	X	E	T
P	O	S	U
S	H	D	E

7 4

Rows: PART, EXIT, SOUP, SHED.
Columns: TIPS, HOAX, SPED,
TRUE. Boxes: TAXI, PERT, SHOP,
DUES.

I	E	U	L
D	W	R	E
T	H	O	M
E	N	S	T

7 5

Rows: LIEU, DREW, MOTH,
SENT. Columns: TIDE, WHEN,
SOUR, MELT. Boxes: WIDE,
RULE, THEN, MOST.

N	S	W	E
E	T	O	D
L	O	C	G
I	F	R	A

7 6

Rows: NEWS, DOTE, CLOG, FAIR.
Columns: LINE, SOFT, CROW,
AGED. Boxes: SENT, OWED,
FOIL, CRAG.

U	G	S	T
C	H	W	E
P	A	E	V
S	N	D	O

7 7

Rows: GUST, CHEW, PAVE, NODS. Columns: CUPS, HANG, WEDS, VOTE. Boxes: CHUG, WEST, SNAP, DOVE.

H	T	W	E
E	N	I	F
L	O	D	A
D	I	N	R

7 8

Rows: WHET, FINE, LOAD, RIND. Columns: HELD, INTO, WIND, FARE. Boxes: THEN, WIFE, IDOL, DARN.

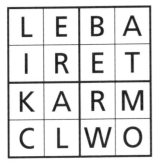

L	E	B	A
I	R	E	T
K	A	R	M
C	L	W	O

7 9

Rows: ABLE, TIRE, MARK, COWL. Columns: LICK, REAL, BREW, MOAT. Boxes: RILE, BEAT, LACK, WORM.

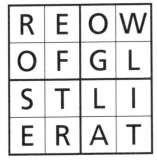

R	E	O	W
O	F	G	L
S	T	L	I
E	R	A	T

8 0

Rows: WORE, GOLF, LIST, RATE. Columns: ROSE, FRET, GOAL, WILT. Boxes: FORE, GLOW, REST, TAIL.

M	E	T	R
U	N	O	D
G	O	E	L
L	D	N	A

8 1

Rows: TERM, UNDO, LOGE, LAND. Columns: GLUM, DONE, TONE, LARD. Boxes: MENU, TROD, GOLD, LEAN.

M	A	D	S
E	C	P	I
U	R	O	F
S	E	N	T

8 2

Rows: DAMS, EPIC, FOUR, SENT. Columns: MUSE, CARE, POND, SIFT. Boxes: CAME, DIPS, SURE, FONT.

W	A	S	G
Y	R	L	E
H	T	A	N
E	N	W	T

8 3

Rows: WAGS, RELY, THAN, WENT. Columns: WHEY, RANT, SLAW, GENT. Boxes: WARY, LEGS, THEN, WANT.

P	D	O	N
E	I	R	H
U	B	N	T
D	R	A	E

8 4

Rows: POND, HIRE, BUNT, READ. Columns: DUPE, BIRD, ROAN, THEN. Boxes: PIED, HORN, DRUB, NEAT.

N	S	A	E
O	W	D	R
R	G	E	W
M	I	T	N

Rows: SANE, WORD, GREW, MINT. Columns: NORM, WIGS, DATE, WREN. Boxes: SNOW, READ, GRIM, WENT.

Y	A	E	R
S	W	H	A
P	I	N	E
R	T	O	S

8 6

Rows: YEAR, WASH, PINE, ROTS. Columns: SPRY, WAIT, HONE, EARS. Boxes: SWAY, HEAR, TRIP, NOSE.

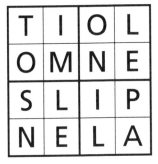

8 7

Rows: TOIL, OMEN, SLIP, LEAN. Columns: TONS, MILE, LION, LEAP. Boxes: OMIT, LONE, LENS, PAIL.

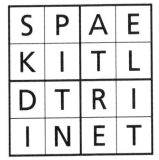

8 8

Rows: APES, KILT, DIRT, TINE. Columns: SKID, PINT, RATE, TILE. Boxes: SKIP, LATE, DINT, TIRE.

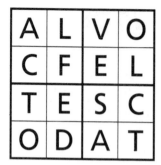

A	L	V	O
C	F	E	L
T	E	S	C
O	D	A	T

89

Rows: OVAL, CLEF, SECT, TOAD.
Columns: COAT, FLED, SAVE, COLT. Boxes: CALF, LOVE, DOTE, CAST.

E	F	A	Z
S	O	G	E
B	S	M	O
A	G	E	R

90

Rows: FAZE, GOES, MOBS, GEAR. Columns: BASE, FOGS, GAME, ZERO. Boxes: FOES, GAZE, BAGS, MORE.

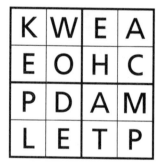

K	W	E	A
E	O	H	C
P	D	A	M
L	E	T	P

91

Rows: WAKE, ECHO, DAMP, PELT. Columns: KELP, OWED, HEAT, CAMP. Boxes: WOKE, EACH, PLED, TAMP.

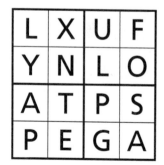

L	X	U	F
Y	N	L	O
A	T	P	S
P	E	G	A

92

Rows: FLUX, ONLY, PAST, PAGE. Columns: PLAY, NEXT, PLUG, SOFA. Boxes: LYNX, FOUL, TAPE, GASP.

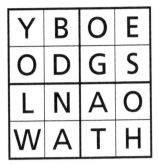

Rows: OBEY, DOGS, LOAN, THAW. Columns: YOWL, BAND, GOAT, HOSE. Boxes: BODY, GOES, LAWN, OATH.

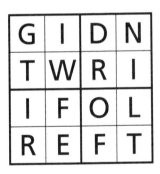

Rows: FAUN, REVS, LAND, SOME. Columns: NOVA, SEND, SLUM, FARE. Boxes: VANE, SURF, NODS, MEAL.

Rows: DING, WRIT, FOIL, FRET. Columns: GRIT, WIFE, FORD, LINT. Boxes: TWIG, RIND, FIRE, LOFT.

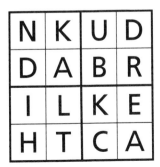

Rows: DUNK, DRAB, LIKE, CHAT. Columns: HIND, TALK, BUCK, READ. Boxes: DANK, DRUB, HILT, CAKE.

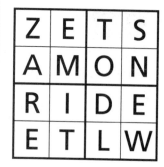

Rows: ZEST, MOAN, RIDE, WELT.
Columns: RAZE, EMIT, TOLD,
NEWS. Boxes: MAZE, TONS,
TIRE, WELD.

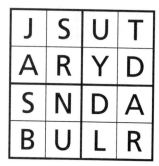

Rows: JUST, YARD, SAND, BLUR.
Columns: JABS, RUNS, DULY,
DART. Boxes: JARS, DUTY,
SNUB, LARD.

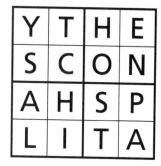

Rows: THEY, CONS, HASP, TAIL.
Columns: LAYS, ITCH, HOST,
PANE. Boxes: CYST, HONE,
HAIL, PAST.

Rows: FAIL, APED, EARS, WINK.
Columns: FANS, LEAK, WIDE,
PAIR. Boxes: LEAF, PAID, SANK,
WIRE.

T	S	G	O
I	W	E	S
W	O	V	A
N	R	I	D

101

Rows: TOGS, WISE, AVOW, RIND. Columns: TWIN, ROWS, GIVE, SODA. Boxes: WITS, GOES, WORN, AVID.

H	P	U	S
O	S	R	E
E	C	O	N
P	A	Y	L

102

Rows: PUSH, SORE, CONE, PLAY. Columns: HOPE, CAPS, YOUR, LENS. Boxes: SHOP, SURE, CAPE, ONLY.

L	A	E	H
C	K	R	O
I	L	A	M
P	E	S	W

103

Rows: HEAL, ROCK, MAIL, PEWS. Columns: CLIP, LAKE, ERAS, WHOM. Boxes: LACK, HERO, PILE, SWAM.

D	A	O	L
E	W	T	P
B	S	U	Y
A	N	R	O

104

Rows: LOAD, WEPT, BUSY, ROAN. Columns: BEAD, SWAN, TOUR, PLOY. Boxes: WADE, PLOT, BANS, YOUR.

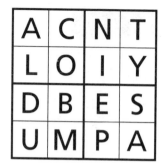

Rows: CANT, OILY, BEDS, PUMA.
Columns: LAUD, COMB, PINE,
STAY. Boxes: COAL, TINY, DUMB,
APES.

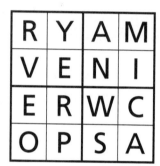

Rows: ARMY, VINE, CREW, SOAP.
Columns: OVER, PREY, SWAN,
MICA. Boxes: VERY, MAIN,
ROPE, CAWS.

Rows: UGLY, SLAP, SUET, RAIN.
Columns: SUIT, LUNG, PAYS,
REAL. Boxes: SLUG, PLAY, UNIT,
EARS.

Rows: POKE, WANT, POND,
MEWS. Columns: PAWN, DOTE,
PEWS, MONK. Boxes: ATOP,
KNEW, WEND, MOPS.

P	O	C	H
E	T	U	M
N	I	L	A
A	R	E	S

1 0 9

Rows: CHOP, MUTE, NAIL, EARS.
Columns: PANE, RIOT, CLUE, MASH. Boxes: POET, MUCH, RAIN, SALE.

A	S	G	E
B	D	O	N
D	O	R	M
L	A	F	I

1 1 0

Rows: SAGE, BOND, DORM, FAIL. Columns: BALD, SODA, FROG, MINE. Boxes: DABS, GONE, LOAD, FIRM.

N	L	I	E
K	A	R	P
J	O	H	S
U	D	E	N

1 1 1

Rows: LINE, PARK, JOSH, DUNE. Columns: JUNK, LOAD, HIRE, PENS. Boxes: LANK, RIPE, JUDO, HENS.

E	H	C	A
R	A	E	V
M	P	I	L
O	R	V	E

1 1 2

Rows: EACH, RAVE, LIMP, OVER. Columns: MORE, HARP, VICE, VEAL. Boxes: HEAR, CAVE, PROM, LIVE.

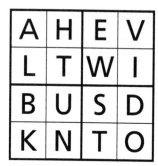

B	I	L	O
N	D	A	S
U	S	R	L
K	H	E	I

1 1 3

Rows: BOIL, SAND, SLUR, HIKE.
Columns: BUNK, DISH, REAL,
SOIL. Boxes: BIND, ALSO,
HUSK, RILE.

A	H	E	V
L	T	W	I
B	U	S	D
K	N	T	O

1 1 4

Rows: HAVE, WILT, BUDS, KNOT.
Columns: BALK, HUNT, WEST,
VOID. Boxes: HALT, VIEW, BUNK,
DOTS.

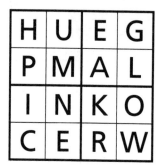

H	U	E	G
P	M	A	L
I	N	K	O
C	E	R	W

1 1 5

Rows: HUGE, PALM, OINK,
CREW. Columns: CHIP, MENU,
RAKE, GLOW. Boxes: HUMP,
GALE, NICE, WORK.

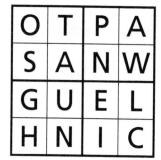

O	T	P	A
S	A	N	W
G	U	E	L
H	N	I	C

1 1 6

Rows: ATOP, SWAN, GLUE, CHIN.
Columns: HOGS, TUNA, PINE,
CLAW. Boxes: OATS, PAWN,
HUNG, LICE.

U	M	E	L
D	R	B	I
F	A	T	S
N	G	L	O

117

Rows: MULE, BIRD, FATS, LONG.
Columns: FUND, GRAM, BELT, SOIL. Boxes: DRUM, BILE, FANG, LOST.

R	E	U	C
O	T	B	L
K	A	N	Y
C	L	M	A

118

Rows: CURE, BOLT, YANK, CALM. Columns: ROCK, LATE, NUMB, CLAY. Boxes: TORE, CLUB, LACK, MANY.

I	P	E	L
R	A	B	O
U	S	T	C
N	G	I	K

119

Rows: PILE, BOAR, CUTS, KING. Columns: RUIN, GASP, BITE, LOCK. Boxes: PAIR, LOBE, SUNG, TICK.

A	P	R	T
G	E	H	U
F	O	E	S
L	K	I	C

120

Rows: PART, HUGE, FOES, LICK. Columns: FLAG, POKE, HIRE, CUTS. Boxes: PAGE, HURT, FOLK, ICES.

N	R	C	O
I	G	E	V
W	I	H	T
S	P	A	L

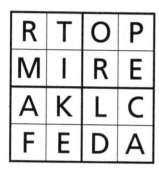

1 2 1

Rows: CORN, GIVE, WITH, SLAP.
Columns: WINS, GRIP, EACH, VOLT. Boxes: GRIN, COVE, WISP, HALT.

R	T	O	P
M	I	R	E
A	K	L	C
F	E	D	A

1 2 2

Rows: PORT, MIRE, LACK, FADE.
Columns: FARM, KITE, LORD, PACE. Boxes: TRIM, ROPE, FAKE, CLAD.

D	R	G	A
O	P	L	E
C	U	S	P
E	B	A	T

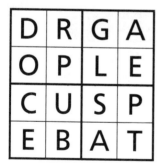

1 2 3

Rows: DRAG, POLE, CUSP, BEAT.
Columns: CODE, BURP, GALS, TAPE. Boxes: PROD, GALE, CUBE, PAST.

H	M	S	U
T	A	K	N
I	R	N	G
C	E	I	S

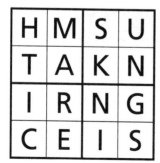

1 2 4

Rows: MUSH, TANK, RING, ICES.
Columns: ITCH, MARE, SKIN, SNUG. Boxes: MATH, SUNK, RICE, SING.

Rows: SLOW, TAKE, SLAP, TIDY.
Columns: WEPT, LIST, LOAD,
YAKS. Boxes: WELT, SOAK, TIPS,
LADY.

W	L	O	S
E	T	A	K
P	S	L	A
T	I	D	Y

1 2 6

Rows: GEAR, TINY, GORE, MAST.
Columns: RENT, GATE, MAYO,
RIGS. Boxes: GENT, AIRY, RATE,
SMOG.

E	G	A	R
N	T	Y	I
R	E	O	G
T	A	M	S

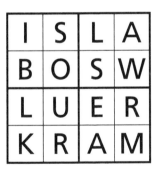

1 2 7

Rows: SAIL, BOWS, RULE,
MARK. Columns: BILK, SOUR,
SALE, WARM. Boxes: BIOS,
LAWS, LURK, MARE.

I	S	L	A
B	O	S	W
L	U	E	R
K	R	A	M

1 2 8

Rows: PUGS, YARN, SITE, BRAT.
Columns: PAYS, RUNT, BASE,
GRIT. Boxes: PUNY, RAGS, STAR,
BITE.

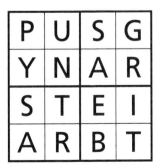

P	U	S	G
Y	N	A	R
S	T	E	I
A	R	B	T

D	E	Z	A
T	B	E	L
A	L	O	C
S	I	D	K

1 2 9

Rows: DAZE, BELT, COAL, KIDS.
Columns: TADS, BILE, DOZE, LACK. Boxes: DEBT, ZEAL, SAIL, DOCK.

B	R	G	A
M	I	L	S
O	F	U	L
T	S	E	B

1 3 0

Rows: BRAG, SLIM, FOUL, BEST.
Columns: TOMB, FIRS, GLUE, SLAB. Boxes: BRIM, LAGS, SOFT, BLUE.

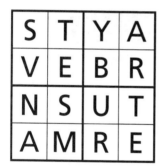

S	T	Y	A
V	E	B	R
N	S	U	T
A	M	R	E

1 3 1

Rows: STAY, VERB, STUN, MARE.
Columns: VANS, STEM, BURY, RATE. Boxes: VEST, BRAY, MANS, TRUE.

H	C	F	E
T	A	L	O
Y	S	A	B
E	N	T	R

1 3 2

Rows: CHEF, ALTO, BAYS, RENT.
Columns: THEY, SCAN, FLAT, ROBE. Boxes: CHAT, FLOE, YENS, BRAT.

N	I	S	P
K	L	W	A
R	F	O	M
I	T	E	L

Rows: SPIN, WALK, FROM, TILE.
Columns: RINK, FLIT, WOES, PALM. Boxes: LINK, PAWS, RIFT, MOLE.

I	L	N	K
T	O	B	U
H	I	R	E
W	R	A	D

1 3 4

Rows: LINK, BOUT, HIRE, DRAW.
Columns: WITH, ROIL, BARN, DUKE. Boxes: TOIL, BUNK, WHIR, READ.

E	N	T	A
L	I	R	E
A	P	E	T
X	E	F	L

1 3 5

Rows: NEAT, RILE, TAPE, FLEX.
Columns: AXLE, PINE, FRET, LATE. Boxes: LINE, RATE, APEX, FELT.

N	Y	A	V
Z	A	H	E
E	L	P	T
O	D	E	N

1 3 6

Rows: NAVY, HAZE, PELT, DONE.
Columns: ZONE, LADY, HEAP, VENT. Boxes: ZANY, HAVE, DOLE, PENT.

137

T	E	N	O
N	X	I	J
C	A	R	S
E	L	U	B

Rows: TONE, JINX, CARS, BLUE.
Columns: CENT, AXLE, RUIN, JOBS. Boxes: NEXT, JOIN, LACE, RUBS.

138

C	H	W	O
P	I	E	R
K	N	B	U
I	D	S	H

Rows: CHOW, PIER, BUNK, DISH. Columns: PICK, HIND, WEBS, HOUR. Boxes: CHIP, WORE, KIND, BUSH.

139

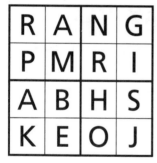

R	A	N	G
P	M	R	I
A	B	H	S
K	E	O	J

Rows: RANG, PRIM, BASH, JOKE. Columns: PARK, BEAM, HORN, JIGS. Boxes: RAMP, GRIN, BAKE, JOSH.

140

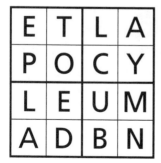

E	T	L	A
P	O	C	Y
L	E	U	M
A	D	B	N

Rows: LATE, COPY, MULE, BAND. Columns: PALE, DOTE, CLUB, MANY. Boxes: POET, CLAY, DEAL, NUMB.

V	Y	A	R
E	B	K	C
N	T	W	A
A	E	H	T

141

Rows: VARY, BECK, WANT, HEAT. Columns: VANE, BYTE, HAWK, CART. Boxes: BEVY, RACK, NEAT, WHAT.

142

Rows: FACT, DIAL, GUYS, TORE. Columns: SODA, CITY, FURL, GATE. Boxes: ACID, FLAT, TOYS, URGE.

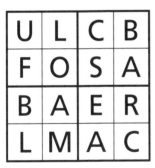

143

Rows: CLUB, SOFA, BEAR, CALM. Columns: FLUB, LOAM, ACES, CRAB. Boxes: FOUL, CABS, BALM, CARE.

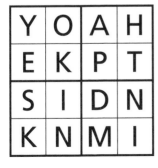

144

Rows: AHOY, KEPT, DINS, MINK. Columns: KEYS, OINK, DAMP, HINT. Boxes: YOKE, PATH, SKIN, MIND.

Rows: GALE, OXEN, FINS, WRAP.
Columns: RING, POSE, FLAX,
ANEW. Boxes: GONE, AXLE,
RIPS, FAWN.

Rows: KNOB, MAYO, HOWL,
SEAT. Columns: MOLE, SOAK,
YAWN, BOTH. Boxes: AMOK,
BONY, SOLE, WHAT.

Rows: JIVE, LAND, ROBS, TOME.
Columns: BOIL, JAMS, DOVE,
RENT. Boxes: JAIL, VEND,
MOBS, TORE.

Rows: SHOT, AUTO, DIME, RANT.
Columns: MOAT, HINT, SODA,
TRUE. Boxes: OATH, OUST,
MINT, READ.

Rows: SNUB, SILK, LOAD, HIDE.
Columns: BIAS, DINE, HULK,
SOLD. Boxes: BINS, SULK, IDEA,
HOLD.

1 5 0

Rows: GEMS, SHUN, BONE,
LAGS. Columns: SONG, BUGS,
SANE, HELM. Boxes: SNUG,
MESH, BOGS, LEAN.

ABOUT THE AUTHORS

ALAN STILLSON's puzzles have appeared in *American Way*, the American Airlines in-flight magazine. He is puzzle editor for Greater Los Angeles Mensa and provides puzzles to local Mensa publications throughout the United States and Canada. His official Mensa puzzle books, *One-Minute Brainteasers*, *Ninety Second Brainteasers*, *Two-Minute Brainteasers*, *The Mensa Genius ABC Quiz Book*, and *Match Wits With Mensa* (coauthored with Marvin Grosswirth and Dr. Abbie F. Salny), continue to delight readers. Other puzzle books include *What's Your CQ?* and *Middle School Word Puzzles*. His puzzles have been reviewed in *People* magazine. Stillson is a member of Mensa, the National Puzzlers League, and the National Scrabble Association.

FRANK LONGO has written more than 45 puzzle books, including more than three dozen sudoku books. Some of his sudoku titles are *The Big Book of Wordoku Puzzles*, the *Mensa® Absolutely Nasty™ Sudoku* series, *Movie-doku*, *The Official Book of Wordoku*, *Oy Vey! Sudoku*, *Sit & Solve® Wordoku*, *Sports-doku*, *Sudoku to Exercise Your Mind*, *10×10 Sudoku*, *TRIVIAL PURSUIT® Sudoku*, *Ultimate Ninja Sudoku*, and *The World's Longest Sudoku Puzzle*. He's also the coauthor of *Mensa® Guide to Solving Sudoku*, *SCRABBLE™-doku*, *The Sudoku Code*, and *Word Search Sudoku*.

WHAT IS MENSA?

Mensa®
The High IQ Society

Mensa is the international society for people with a high IQ. We have more than 100,000 members in over 40 countries world-wide.

The society's aims are:
- to identify and foster human intelligence for the benefit of humanity;
- to encourage research in the nature, characteristics, and uses of intelligence;
- to provide a stimulating intellectual and social environment for its members.

Anyone with an IQ score in the top two percent of the population is eligible to become a member of Mensa—are you the "one in 50" we've been looking for?

Mensa membership offers an excellent range of benefits:
- Networking and social activities nationally and around the world;
- Special Interest Groups (hundreds of chances to pursue your hobbies and interests—from art to zoology!);
- Monthly International Journal, national magazines, and regional newsletters;
- Local meetings—from game challenges to food and drink;
- National and international weekend gatherings and conferences;
- Intellectually stimulating lectures and seminars;
- Access to the worldwide SIGHT network for travelers and hosts.

For more information about Mensa International:
www.mensa.org
Telephone: +44 1400 272675
e-mail: enquiries@mensa.org
Mensa International Ltd.
Slate Barn
Church Lane
Caythorpe, Lincolnshire NG32 3EL
United Kingdom

For more information about American Mensa:
www.us.mensa.org
Telephone: 1-800-66-MENSA
American Mensa Ltd.
1229 Corporate Drive West
Arlington, TX 76006-6103 USA

For more information about British Mensa (UK and Ireland):
www.mensa.org.uk
Telephone: +44 (0) 1902 772771
e-mail: enquiries@mensa.org.uk
British Mensa Ltd.
St. John's House
St. John's Square
Wolverhampton WV2 4AH
United Kingdom

For more information about Australian Mensa:
www.mensa.org.au
Telephone: +61 1902 260 594
e-mail: info@mensa.org.au
Australian Mensa Inc.
PO Box 212
Darlington WA 6070 Australia

ALLOWABLE WORDS

```
ABED AWLS BLAH BUSY CLOY CZAR DONE EPIC FLOG GERM HAIL HOPE JIBS LAMP
ABET AWOL BLED BUTS CLUB DABS DONG ERAS FLOP GEST HAIR HOPS JIGS LAMS
ABLE AWRY BLEW BUYS CLUE DACE DONS ERGO FLOW GETS HAKE HORA JILT LAND
ABLY AXED BLIP BYES COAL DADS DOPE ERGS FLUB GIBE HALE HORN JINX LANE
ABUT AXEL BLOC BYTE COAT DAHS DOPY ESPY FLUE GIFT HALF HOSE JIVE LANK
ACED AXES BLOG CABS COAX DAFT DORK ETAS FLUS GILD HALO HOST JOBS LAPS
ACES AXIS BLOT CADS COBS DAIS DORM ETCH FLUX GILT HALT HOTS JOCK LARD
ACHE AXLE BLOW CAFE CODA DALE DORY EURO FOAL GIMP HAMS HOUR JOEY LARK
ACHY AXON BLUE CAGE CODE DAME DOSE EVIL FOAM GINS HAND HOVE JOGS LASH
ACID AYES BLUR CAGY CODS DAMN DOTE EXAM FOBS GIRD HANG HOWL JOHN LAST
ACME BACK BOAR CAKE COED DAMP DOTS EXIT FOCI GIRL HANK HUBS JOIN LATE
ACNE BADE BOAS CAKY COGS DAMS DOUR EXPO FOES GIRT HAPS HUED JOKE LATH
ACRE BAGS BOAT CALF COIF DANG DOVE FACE FOGS GIST HARD HUES JOLT LATS
ACTS BAHT BOCK CALM COIL DANK DOWN FACT FOGY GIVE HARE HUGE JOSH LAUD
ADOS BAIL BODE CAME COIN DARE DOZE FADE FOIL GLAD HARK HUGS JOTS LAVE
ADZE BAIT BODS CAMO COKE DARK DRAB FADS FOLD GLAM HARM HULA JOWL LAVS
AEON BAKE BODY CAMP COLA DARN DRAG FAIL FOLK GLEN HARP HULK JOYS LAWN
AGED BALD BOGS CAMS COLD DART DRAM FAIN FOND GLIB HART HUMP JUDO LAWS
AGES BALE BOGY CANE COLE DASH DRAT FAIR FONT GLOB HASP HUMS JUGS LAYS
AGIN BALK BOIL CANS COLT DATE DRAW FAKE FOPS GLOM HATE HUNG JUKE LAZE
AGUE BALM BOLD CANT COMA DAUB DRAY FAME FORA GLOP HATS HUNK JUMP LAZY
AHEM BAND BOLT CAPE COMB DAWN DREW FANG FORD GLOW HAUL HUNS JUNK LEAD
AHOY BANE BOND CAPO COME DAYS DRIP FANS FORE GLUE HAVE HUNT JURY LEAF
AIDE BANG BONE CAPS COMP DAZE DROP FARE FORK GLUM HAWK HURL JUST LEAK
AIDS BANK BONG CARB CONE DEAF DRUB FARM FORM GLUT HAWS HURT JUTE LEAN
AILS BANS BONK CARD CONN DEAL DRUG FARO FORT GNAT HAYS HUSK JUTS LEAP
AIMS BARD BONY CARE CONS DEAN DRUM FAST FOUL GNAW HAZE HUTS KALE LEAS
AIRS BARE BOPS CARP CONY DEAR DUAL FATE FOUR GNUS HAZY HYMN KART LEFT
AIRY BARK BORE CARS COPE DEBS DUBS FATS FOWL GOAD HEAD HYPE KAYO LEGS
AKIN BARN BORN CART COPS DEBT DUCK FAUN FOXY GOAL HEAL HYPO KAYS LEIS
ALES BARS BOSH CASE COPY DECK DUCT FAUX FRAT GOAT HEAP IAMB KEGS LEKS
ALIT BASE BOTH CASH CORD DEFT DUEL FAVE FRAY GOBS HEAR IBEX KELP LEND
ALMS BASH BOTS CASK CORE DEFY DUES FAWN FRET GODS HEAT ICED KENO LENS
ALOE BASK BOUT CAST CORK DELI DUET FAZE FROG GOER HECK ICES KENS LENT
ALPS BATE BOWL CATS CORM DELT DUKE FEAR FROM GOES HEFT ICKY KEPI LEST
ALSO BATH BOWS CAVE CORN DEMO DULY FEAT FRUG GOLD HEIR ICON KEPT LETS
ALTO BATS BOXY CAWS COST DENS DUMB FELT FUEL GONE HELD IDEA KERB LEVY
ALUM BAUD BOYS CAYS COSY DENY DUMP FEND FUME GONG HELM IDES KEYS LEWD
AMEN BAWD BRAD CELS COTE DESK DUNE FENS FUND GORE HELP IDLE KHAN LIAR
AMID BAWL BRAE CENT COTS DEWS DUNG FERN FUNK GORY HEMP IDLY KIDS LIBS
AMOK BAYS BRAG CHAD COUP DEWY DUNS FETA FURL GOSH HEMS IDOL KILN LICE
AMPS BEAD BRAN CHAI COVE DIAL DUOS FEUD FURS GOUT HENS IDYL KILO LICK
ANDS BEAK BRAS CHAP COWL DIBS DUSK FIAT FURY GOWN HERB ILKS KILT LIDS
ANEW BEAM BRAT CHAR COWS DICE DUST FIBS FUSE GRAB HERD IMPS KIND LIED
ANIL BEAN BRAY CHAT COZY DIES DUTY FIGS FUZE GRAD HERO INCH KINE LIEF
ANKH BEAR BRED CHAW CRAB DIET DYER FILE FUZZ GRAM HERS INFO KING LIEN
ANTE BEAT BREW CHEF CRAG DIGS DYES FILM GABS GRAN HEWN INKS KINS LIES
ANTI BEAU BRIG CHEW CRAM DIKE DYNE FIND GADS GRAY HEWS INKY KIPS LIEU
ANTS BECK BRIM CHIN CRAW DIME EACH FINE GAIN GREW HICK INTO KITE LIFE
APED BEDS BRIO CHIP CRED DIMS EARL FINK GAIT GREY HIDE IONS KITH LIFT
APES BEGS BRIS CHIS CREW DINE EARN FINS GALE GRID HIED IOTA KITS LIKE
APEX BELT BROS CHIT CRIB DING EARS FIRE GALS GRIM HIES IRES KNEW LIMB
APSE BEND BROW CHOP CROP DINS EASY FIRM GAME GRIN HIKE IRKS KNIT LIME
ARCH BENT BRUT CHOW CROW DINT EATS FIRS GAMS GRIP HILT IRON KNOB LIMN
ARCS BERG BUCK CHUB CRUD DIPS EAVE FISH GAMY GRIT HIND ITCH KNOT LIMO
ARES BERM BUDS CHUG CRUX DIRE EBBS FIST GAOL GROK HINT ITEM KNOW LIMP
ARID BEST BUGS CHUM CUBE DIRK ECHO FITS GAPE GROW HIPS JABS KOAN LINE
ARKS BETA BULK CIAO CUBS DIRT ECRU FIVE GAPS GRUB HIRE JADE KOLA LINK
ARMS BETS BUMP CIGS CUED DISC EDDY FLAB GARB GULF HITS JAGS LABS LINT
ARMY BEVY BUMS CINE CUES DISH EDGY FLAG GARS GULP HIVE JAIL LACE LION
ARTS BEYS BUNG CITE CUKE DISK EDIT FLAK GASH GUMS HOAR JAMB LACK LIPS
ARTY BIAS BUNK CITY CULT DITZ EFTS FLAN GASP GUNK HOAX JAMS LACS LIRA
ARUM BIDE BUNS CLAD CUPS DIVA EGAD FLAP GATE GUNS HOBO JANE LACY LIRE
ASHY BIDS BUNT CLAM CURB DIVE EGIS FLAT GATS GUSH HODS JAPE LADE LISP
ATOM BIER BUOY CLAN CURD DOCK EGOS FLAW GAUD GUST HOED JARL LADS LIST
ATOP BIKE BURG CLAP CURE DOCS ELAN FLAX GAWK GUTS HOER JARS LADY LIVE
AUKS BILE BURL CLAW CURL DOER ELKS FLAY GAYS GUYS HOES JAYS LAGS LOAD
AUNT BILK BURN CLAY CURS DOES ELMS FLEA GAZE GYMS HOGS JEAN LAIC LOAF
AUTO BIND BURP CLEF CURT DOGE EMIR FLED GEAR GYPS HOLD JEEP LAID LOAM
AVER BINS BURS CLIP CUSP DOGS EMIT FLEW GELD GYRO HOLE JERK LAIN LOAN
AVID BIOS BURY CLOD CUTE DOIT EMUS FLEX GELS HACK HOLY JEST LAIR LOBE
AVOW BIRD BUSH CLOG CUTS DOLT ENDS FLIP GELT HADJ HOME JETS LAKE LOBS
AWED BITE BUSK CLOP CYAN DOME ENVY FLIT GEMS HAFT HONE JIBB LAMB LOCH
AWES BITS BUST CLOT CYST DONA EONS FLOE GENT HAGS HONK JIBE LAME LOCI
```

```
LOCK MEGS NAPE ORAL PICA PULI RIFT SANG SLID STUD THUD TYPO WANT WOLD
LODE MELD NAPS ORBS PICK PUMA RIGS SANK SLIM STUN THUG TYRE WARD WOLF
LOFT MELT NARC ORCA PICS PUNK RILE SARI SLIP STYE THUS TYRO WARE WOMB
LOGE MEND NARK ORES PIED PUNS RIME SATE SLIT SUCH TICK TZAR WARM WONK
LOGS MENU NARY ORGY PIER PUNT RIMS SAVE SLOB SUCK TICS UDON WARN WONT
LOGY MEOW NAVE OUCH PIES PUNY RIMY SAWN SLOE SUED TIDE UGHS WARP WORD
LOIN MESA NAVY OURS PIGS PURE RIND SCAB SLOG SUET TIDY UGLY WARS WORE
LONE MESH NAYS OUST PIKE PURL RING SCAM SLOP SUIT TIED UKES WART WORK
LONG METH NEAP OUTS PILE PUSH RINK SCAN SLOT SULK TIER ULNA WARY WORM
LOPE MEWL NEAR OVAL PINE PUTS RIOT SCAR SLOW SUMO TIES UMPS WASH WORN
LOPS MEWS NEAT OVEN PING PYRE RIPE SCAT SLUE SUMP TILE UNDO WASP WORT
LORD MICA NEBS OVER PINK PYRO RIPS SCOW SLUG SUNG TIME UNIT WAVE WOVE
LORE MICE NECK OVUM PINS QUAD RISE SCUM SLUM SUNK TINE UNTO WAVY WRAP
LORN MICS NERD OWED PINT QUAY RISK SEAL SLUR SURE TINS UPDO WAXY WREN
LOSE MIEN NEST OWES PINY QUID RITE SEAM SMOG SURF TINY UPON WAYS WRIT
LOST MIKE NETS OWLS PITA QUIP RIVE SEAR SMUG SWAB TIPS URGE WEAK WYES
LOTS MILD NEWS PACE PITH QUIT ROAD SEAT SMUT SWAG TIRE URNS WEAL YAKS
LOUD MILE NEWT OXEN PITS QUIZ ROAM SECT SNAG SWAM TOAD USED WEAN YAMS
LOUT MILK NEXT PACE PITY RACE ROAN SELF SNAP SWAN TOED USER WEAR YANG
LOVE MILS NIBS PACK PIXY RACK ROBE SEMI SNIP SWAP TOES UTES WEBS YANK
LOWS MIND NICE PACT PLAN RACY ROBS SEND SNIT SWAT TOFU UVEA WEDS YAPS
LUBE MINE NICK PADS PLAY RADS ROCK SENT SNOB SWAY TOGA VAIN WEFT YARD
LUCK MINK NIGH PAGE PLEA RAFT ROCS SERA SNOW SWIG TOGS VALE WEIR YARN
LUGE MINT NIPS PAID PLED RAGE RODE SERF SNUB SWIM TOIL VAMP WELD YAWL
LUGS MINX NITE PAIL PLIE RAGS RODS SEWN SNUG SWUM TOKE VANE WELT YAWN
LUMP MIRE NITS PAIN PLOD RAID ROES SEXY SOAK SYNC TOLD VANS WEND YAWP
LUNG MISO NODE PAIR PLOT RAIL ROIL SHAD SOAP TABS TOMB VARY WENS YAWS
LUNK MIST NODS PALE PLOW RAIN ROLE SHAG SOAR TABU TOME VASE WENT YEAH
LURE MITE NOEL PALM PLOY RAKE ROMP SHAM SOBA TACH TOMS VAST WEPT YEAR
LURK MOAN NOES PALS PLUG RAMP ROPE SHAY SOCK TACK TONE VATS WEST YEAS
LUSH MOAT NOIR PANE PLUM RAMS ROPY SHED SODA TACO TONS VEAL WETS YELP
LUST MOBS NOPE PANG PLUS RAND ROSE SHIM SOFA TADS TONY VEIL WHAM YENS
LUTE MOCK NORM PANS POCK RANG ROSY SHIN SOFT TAGS TOPS VEIN WHAP YETI
LYES MOCS NOSE PANT PODS RANI ROTE SHIP SOIL TAIL TORE VEND WHAT YEWS
LYNX MODE NOSH PARD POEM RANK ROTS SHIV SOLD TAKE TORI VENT WHEN YINS
LYRE MODS NOSY PARE POET RANT ROUE SHOD SOLE TALC TORN VERB WHET YIPS
MACE MOIL NOTE PARK POIS RAPS ROUT SHOE SOLI TALE TORS VERY WHEY YIPS
MACH MOLD NOVA PART POKE RAPT ROUX SHOP SOME TALK TOSH VEST WHIM YOGA
MACS MOLE NUBS PASS POKY RASH ROVE SHOT SONG TAME TOUR VETO WHIP YOGI
MADE MOLT NUDE PAST POLE RASP ROWS SHOW SOPH TAMP TOWN VETS WHIR YOKE
MAGS MONK NUKE PATE POLS RATE RUBE SHUL SORE TAMS TOWS VIAL WHIT YOLK
MAID MOPE NUMB PATH POME RATS RUBS SHUN SORT TANG TOYS VIBE WHIZ YORE
MAIL MOPS NUTS PATS POND RAVE RUBY SHUT SOUL TANK TRAM VICE WHOA YOUR
MAIN MOPY OAFS PAVE PONE RAYS RUDE SICK SOUP TANS TRAP VIED WHOM YOWL
MAKE MORE OAKS PAWL PORE RAZE RUED SIDE SOUR TAPE TRAY VIER WHOP YUAN
MAKO MORN OARS PAWN PORK READ RUES SIFT SOWN TAPS TREF VIES WHYS YUKS
MALE MOSH OATH PAWS PORN REAL RUGS SIGH SOYA TARE TREK VIEW WICK YULE
MALT MOST OATS PAYS PORT REAM RUIN SIGN SPAM TARO TREY VILE WIDE YURT
MANE MOTE OBEY PEAK POSE REAP RULE SILK SPAN TARP TRIG VIMS WIDE ZAPS
MANS MOTH OBIS PEAL POSH REBS RUMP SILO SPAR TARS TRIM VINE WIFE ZAGS
MANY MOTS OBIT PEAR POST REDO RUMS SILT SPAT TASK TRIO VINO WIGS ZANY
MAPS MOUE ODES PEAS POSY REDS RUNG SIMP SPAY TAUS TRIP VIOL WILD ZAPS
MARE MOVE OGLE PEAT POTS REFS RUNS SINE SPEC TAXI TROD VISA WILE ZEAL
MARK MOWN OGRE PECK POUR REGS RUNT SING SPED TEAK TROY VISE WILT ZEBU
MARS MOWS OHMS PECS POUT REIN RUSE SINK SPEW TEAL TRUE VOID WILY ZEDS
MART MUCH OILS PEDS POWS RELY RUSK SIRE SPIN TEAM TSAR VOLE WIMP ZERO
MASH MUCK OILY PEGS PRAM REMS RUST SITE SPIT TEAR TUBA VOLT WIND ZEST
MASK MUDS OINK PELF PRAT REND RUTS SIZE SPOT TEAS TUBE VOTE WINE ZETA
MAST MUGS OKAY PELT PRAY RENT RYES SKEW SPRY TECH TUBS VOWS WING ZIGS
MATE MULE OKRA PEND PREY REPO SACK SKID SPUD TEMP TUCK WADE WINK ZINC
MATH MURK OLDS PENS PREZ REPS SAFE SKIM SPUN TEND TUGS WADI WINO ZINE
MATS MUSE OLES PENT PRIG REST SAGA SKIN SPUR TENS TUNA WADS WINS ZING
MAUL MUSH OMEN PEON PRIM REVS SAGE SKIP STAB TERM TUNE WAFT WIPE ZIPS
MAWS MUSK OMIT PERK PROD RHEA SAGO SKIT STAG TERN TURF WAGE WIRE ZITS
MAXI MUST ONCE PERM PROF RHOS SAID SLAB STAR THAN TURN WAGS WIRY ZONE
MAYO MUTE ONES PERT PROM RIAL SAIL SLAG STAY THAW TUSH WAIF WISE ZONK
MAZE MYNA ONLY PESO PROS RIBS SALE SLAM STEM THEM TUSK WAIL WISH ZORI
MAZY MYTH ONUS PEST PROW RICE SAKE SLAP STEP THEN TWAS WAIT WISP
MEAD NABS ONYX PETS PUBS RICH SALT SLAT STEW THEY TWIG WAKE WITH
MEAL NAGS OPAL PEWS PUCE RICK SALE SLAW STIR THIN TWIN WALE WITS
MEAN NAIF OPEN PHAT PUCK RIDE SAME SLAY STOP THIS TWOS WALK WOES
MEAT NAIL OPTS PHEW PUGS RIDS SAND SLED STOW THOU TYKE WAND WOKE
MEDS NAME OPUS PHIS PULE RIFE SANE SLEW STUB THRU TYPE WANE WOKS
```

128